# In My Father's Arms

## Jozelle L. Mator

In My Father's Arms
Published by Kingdom Publishing, LLC
Odenton, Maryland U.S.A.

Printed in the U.S.A.

Unless otherwise indicated, all Scripture quotations are taken from the King James Version of the Holy Bible (Public Domain). Scripture quotations noted AMPLIFIED or AMP are taken from the Amplified® Bible, copyright © 1954, 1958, 1962, 1964, 1965, 1987 by the Lockman Foundation. Used by permission (www.Lockman.org).

Library of Congress Control Number: 2020908542

Paperback ISBN: 978-1-947741-55-3
Ebook ISBN: 978-1-947741-56-0

# ACKNOWLEDGEMENTS

I would like to thank all of the amazing people that The Lord so strategically placed in my life and on my path thus far as I've been in the process of being molded more and more into His likeness:

My husband, whose presence in my life is added confirmation that striving to wait on the Lord is never in vain.

My mother and father, who defied all odds as survivors of a devastating civil war, overcame all obstacles and never failed to ensure that I was raised in the admonition of the Lord.

My brother and sister-in law, two of my biggest supporters and encouragers.

My personal divine helpers and my spiritual parents who have all helped direct, mold, educate and mentor me in various seasons of my growth in Christ, thus far.

My best friend and my sisters in Christ, who have held my hand, grown and evolved with me through the hills and valleys of our individual journeys, thus far.

My family and friends who have added authentic love, support, laughter and joy to my life.

*God Bless each and every one of you!*

# TABLE OF CONTENT

# FOREWORD

This book, In My Father's Arms, is extremely informative. Jozelle was able to articulate her heart and at the same time take me on a journey of discovering our will verses the will of God. In My Father's Arms reminded me of the biblical literacy it takes to stay grounded in faith. Heaven and earth will pass away but the word of God will remain forever. This book causes the scriptures to be alive and active in deliverance. Jozelle detailed her desire for us all to depend on the Lord and the accountability it takes for transformaation. I pray everyone who reads this great book will find hope, peace, joy and comfort. In everything, I pray you come to the conclusion, as I did, that God's arms are big enough to hold the whole world, yet loving and close enough that you feel like you're the only person in the world.

Jozelle, thank you for sharing all that our Heavenly Father is able to accomplish in our lives.

Love you and God bless you tremendously,

*Lady Sandra Dickens*
New Wine Worship Center
York, PA

# INTRODUCTION

Our Heavenly Father, in all His infinite wisdom, has such a strategic way of allowing us to reach our breaking point with the sole purpose of rebuilding us His way, for His glory. Taking our circumstances, our poor decisions, our heartbreaks and our confusion and allowing it all to bring us to a place of total surrender unto to Him.

## Gracefully Broken

Now don't be misled, that process doesn't always feel good and if you're anything like me, not being able to have control over the process can even feel like physical pain, at times.

Yet, how can God truly be God in our lives, if we're constantly trying to play His role?

It's in that season of breaking that the Lord begins the rebirthing process of rebuilding us into a new creation, His new creation, from the inside, out.

> *Therefore if anyone is in Christ [that is, grafted in, joined to Him by faith in Him as Savior], he is a new creature [reborn and renewed by the Holy Spirit]; the old things [the previous moral and spiritual condition] have passed away. Behold, new things have come [because spiritual awakening brings a new life]*
> **2 Corinthians 5:17 AMP**

It's in that time of complete and utter vulnerability that our Creator begins the process of showing us who we truly are, why we are here on this earth, and who we are called to be. It is in that season that He begins pruning us of the things that are not pleasing to Him, do not honor and represent Him and stretching us to take us from where we were and are, to where He desires for us to be; where He planned for us to be all along.

It is in that life-changing encounter that our Savior begins molding us more and more into His likeness, and despite our shortcomings, showering us with the most incredible, undeniable, and unconditional love that we will *ever* receive.

## Total Surrender

Many of us tend to have already developed a plan or idea, in our minds, of how we believe things should come together in our lives. For example, we may read the scripture:

*A man's heart plans his way [as he journeys through life], But the LORD determines his steps and establishes them*
**Proverbs 16:9 AMP**

We can attest to the first part because we know for a fact that it's accurate. The second part, well, let's just say that more times than not, our first instinct and desire is for the Lord to determine our steps according to how our hearts have already planned them.

*Right?*

Sorry to be the bearer of "bad" news, but the Almighty and all-knowing God certainly doesn't operate on our times table; and with *good* reason! I personally had to learn this the hard way, though.

It took doing things my way, the wrong way, for so long that I found myself at my wits end, completely heartbroken, confused by life in general and at my ultimate lowest. That is when I literally and physically came to the point where I threw up my hands and screamed... "**This** just cannot be **life**, God; there has *got to be* a better way than **this**, Lord!"

Repeatedly spinning my wheels had gotten me nowhere that I *thought* I should've been, but it did get me to the very place God needed me to be all along:

*Ready to surrender absolutely everything to Him!*

---

I've made *many* mistakes along the way, thus far. I have fallen short many times but by the grace of God I have gotten back up, every single time and I have never looked back with a desire to turn back because so far, as trying as the journey has been at times, there was truly nothing desirable enough to look back to that ever truly gave me the peace that my heart, mind and soul yearns for!

You see, God could have literally left me in my own confusion and I could've just continued with the façade that I had it all together yet remained so torn from within until the worst could have occurred--*but God!* He had a different plan, a plan to use my life to paint a beautiful picture of His love.

As many people as I had surrounding me, my family and friends that love me with all that they have, the fact is that *only* God could see the truest state of my heart and mind.

Only God could see my brokenness from within, and it was only He who had the ability to fix it. He knew just what to do and the process it would take to accomplish it; the breaking and the rebuilding that would be required.

Like Maxwell the R&B musician sang, *"I was reborn, when I was broken."*

That line always stuck out to me when I heard his song play because I could so easily apply it to my own situation, spiritually. Indeed, I too was reborn, for I was reborn *in Christ Jesus* and the

Lord knew that it all *had* to be dealt with if His purpose for my life would ever be fulfilled.

People say, yell and post on social media and various other platforms that "God is Faithful", all the time.

It holds true weight and real meaning though, when we realize and recognize just how mightily we've experienced His faithfulness.

It is my most sincere hope that you don't wait until you get to your 'wits end' to identify your need for your Heavenly Father, *but* if you find yourself in that position, it is my prayer that as you follow my journey by way of my story and selected journal entries and as you read the words in the following pages, you will be reminded and encouraged that it is never too late to build or rebuild your personal relationship with Jesus Christ-- that you are encouraged to take up your cross and devote yourself to the most amazing journey you will ever experience--your journey with your Savior.

I pray that the story of my discovery of God's truth simply inspires you to realize and recognize it for yourself if you haven't already; that your love and understanding of God and His Word will in fact drop from just your *head*, to your *heart* because more than anything else, I realized that by the grace of God, once my *heart* actually changed, is when my *life* began to!

He is always waiting with open arms. It's no coincidence that everything I once felt I lacked, and everything that I thought I lost, was found…

… In My Father's Arms.

# WHEN GOD STEPS IN

It was Winter, 2010 and I was 23 years old.

I was in a place in my life where I was still emotionally and mentally drained, tired of what felt like running in circles yet never quite getting anywhere purposeful and still completely overtaken by heartbreak from years prior, no matter how much I strived to mask it. I was living just as anyone else my age was, or so I thought. I was in college, and when many of my friends and classmates weren't in class, studying, or working, things like partying and drinking, as well as all the experiences and encounters that they can potentially lead to, became the norm. It was all around me and quickly became typical for me as well and to be honest, at that time, nothing about any of it seemed or even felt wrong. It had become what I was used to, accustomed to and comfortable with. It was how most people I knew chose to wind down after a long day at work, or a long week at school. Balancing the stress of college, juggling and maintaining friendships and relationships, as well as keeping up with the possible demands of our jobs was rough at times, therefore the ways in which many of us chose to balance it all out felt like it was all well deserved. I must say that many laughs were shared, and many bonds were formed during this unforgettable season of my life. Some bonds only lasted for a short period of time and resulted in lessons learned, and others, God allowed to withstand the tests of time.

I had yet to experience the true conviction that comes from the Holy Spirit because I didn't have a personal relationship with the Lord, yet.

Yes, *on the surface*, everything looked as though it was as it should be, especially when surrounded by those who were involved in the very same things that brought me laughter and temporary happiness.

It's only God who can truly see beyond the surface. He is fully aware of what's really going on inside. He knows all, He sees all and that is why there is no one on this earth that could ever compare to Him!

He was aware of all that I used to subconsciously and sometimes even intentionally involve myself in to avoid having to deal with what was really going on from within.

*Just 2 years prior, in 2008,* I was on my college campus, stuck in myself, in my dorm room, by choice, silently battling what I was later diagnosed with as *Situational Depression.* For weeks at a time I didn't leave my campus townhome (let's just say, my grades that semester were the worse I ever had!) due to experiencing the most unexplainable anxiety and fear. None of it made sense to me, but it was my reality. My roommate at the time worked night shift and slept during the day before her evening classes, which simply suited my struggle because I was able to freely move about in our townhome all day and night with no questions asked. I stayed awake night after night and distinctly remember standing in the shower for hours at a time, every single night, trying to envision Heaven and what I thought it would look like - *for hours,* until the hot water finally turned cold and I stepped out of the shower with my body covered in wrinkles - literally, *every single night.* I remember that for some reason I felt completely convinced (which I much later realized was the work of the enemy) that Heaven was not only my very next destination but that I'd be arriving there, shortly. Every night, for months, I would repeatedly dream about walking through a graveyard, back and forth, passing hundreds of tombstones. Nothing would happen; I would just aimlessly wander in the dark throughout the entire dream.

My parents realized that they hadn't seen me for a couple weeks at a time, but I simply covered it up by telling them that I was working on the weekends to save up some money. They accepted it, but I could tell that they weren't fully convinced.

*Attentive parents tend to notice everything.*

My father began to send me daily devotionals via e-mail every single day and for the moment they gave me great glimmers of hope because at the time, I was trying to cope with a break-up that led to a heartbreak that I just could not seem to get over. It felt like a true battle because I had never experienced heartbreak ever before. I had given every ounce of what I knew how to give at that time, and it resulted in me feeling utterly rejected and completely drained. I literally felt like a vehicle on "E," unable to move forward... *just stuck*. I didn't know where to regain the strength that I needed to go on. Around the same time, I was also silently struggling with the death of my uncle. It was difficult for my entire family, and not only was I already at my weakest from emotional pain that was taking a toll on my body as well, but I had also never experienced the death of anyone truly close to me. I had difficulty comprehending it and I had absolutely no clue what to do with all of my emotions, so I kept them bottled up inside. It felt like the easiest thing to do at the time because even at that age, it didn't seem as if people outside of my immediate family expected *me* to have "issues." I was convinced that some may have felt as though I may have been too privileged to have any, and many others may have just assumed that I always had it together because I always had a smile on my face and a listening ear for others. It just came naturally and I later came to realize that, yes indeed, that natural listening ear and authentic heart for others is one of the greatest gifts God has blessed me with, but it surely didn't mean that I would ever be exempt from my own trials and tribulations. Still, at that time, I practically felt guilty for admitting that I had any struggles, so I chose to keep them to myself.

*"Sometimes, the prettiest smiles hide the deepest secrets. The brightest eyes have cried the most tears. The kindest hearts have felt the most pain"* - Author Unknown

Yes, I knew of the importance of praying about it, but I didn't yet know what that truly meant; I didn't know how to *cast all my cares upon God* (1 Peter 5:7).

Now, Satan is always lurking, and the fact is, he was very well aware of my struggles. I had allowed myself to be so open and accessible to him; I became a perfect target. I had become so *distant from Christ* and indulged in a slew of sins that I'm sure I was committing both knowingly and unknowingly. The enemy knew this, took advantage of it and he used that moment to pounce.

It took me a while to understand and accept that as a child of God, the Lord never promised that weapons would not form, He simply and clearly stated, that by His grace, they would not prosper!

*No weapon that is formed against you shall succeed; and every tongue that rises against you in judgment you will condemn. This [peace, righteousness, security, and triumph over opposition] is the heritage of the servants of the Lord, and this is their vindication from Me," says the LORD.*
**Isaiah 54:17 AMP**

Through this, I learned that If God *allowed* the weapons to form, there is a strategic plan and purpose for it. Just as the Word of God states, He does *not* have plans to see us fail, for His plan is not to harm us but to give us hope, future and an expected end (Jeremiah 29:11-13).

The Lord had to allow me to experience the attack in order to bring to light how un-sturdy my foundation was, for it was not built on Him, The Rock of Ages. He had to ensure that going forth, I would understand the vitality of truly staying connected to Him; The Vine.

*New Year's Eve 2008,* I was now home from school on Christmas vacation. I was trying my absolute best to keep a smile on my face for friends and family but feeling the most uneasy that I had ever felt, to date. I was experiencing true and authentic anxiety and as my family and I sat in the living room watching MTV as the ball dropped and the clock struck 12am midnight, the New Year 2009 officially began. A time when we are usually dancing, singing, praising and worshipping God as a family for another year, I was curled up in the corner of our living room couch, physically shaking out of pure fear, tears streaming down my face. I could no longer keep it in, it could no longer be a secret; it was all too obvious and for the first time I was forced out of absolute terror from within, to express to my parents:

> *"I feel like I'm going to die.*
> *I think this is the end for me.*
> *I don't know why or what to do."*

This began the year-long process of my parents doing everything it took to seek help for me and with me. I first spoke with the Pastors of the Lutheran Church that I grew up in, and though everything they poured into me truly helped put things into proper perspective, I still had no personal relationship with the Lord, and Satan continued to attack. He knew that I was unable to spiritually fight back by allowing God to fight for me.

My mother has always taken a "whatever it takes" approach to things and though this may not have been what they had preferred, and though my father was not in favor of it at first, he finally agreed, and they encouraged me to seek a psychiatrist.

Yes, that experience was a blessing as well; it gave me the opportunity to express myself to someone who knew nothing about me previously, had no assumptions, no bias and whom I could be freely open and honest with.

The issue came when I was diagnosed with Situational Depression and was prescribed medication. It may have been because I was very inconsistent and careless at that age and stage of my life, or possibly that I felt I could overcome my struggle without medicine, but it was probably a little bit of both. I am not a medical professional and I would *never* recommend the medication that is prescribed by professional doctors not to be taken, but I must admit that I am guilty of taking the medication that was prescribed to me, only once.

A few months later, I met *Warkedia*.

*This was truly an encounter with one of my personal "divine helpers."* A true shift of the entire course of my life was about to occur.

It was now winter, 2010. I was still in college and I also worked at a nursing home on the night shift which gave me a lot of down time. Enough time to properly take care of my residents, tend to all of their needs, and it also gave me enough time to *think*.

Initially, when I met Warkedia she was simply just another coworker working the night shift with me. I've always been told that I'm a pretty easy person to get along with and hold meaningful conversations with, so it was of no surprise that we quickly went from discussing patients, to also discussing life, in general.

The one thing about Warkedia that stood out to me the most was that she kept it *real*. She was so transparent. The more we talked, the more she opened up about her own past, her struggles of growing up in Baltimore, Maryland and the hardships she endured as a woman in the world, living on the wrong side of the tracks and making poor decisions that resulted in consequences with lasting scars. Though our stories differed in various ways, her authenticity drew me in and I wanted to hear more about her battles and how she overcame them because she spoke about them, not out of shame, but out of an undeniable joy that exuded from within her. Soon, she began to share with me how The Lord had not only been working in and through her life from the inside out. Even though she had made many mistakes and found herself in some of the worst predicaments, He has never given up on her. His love for her gave her a whole new perspective and it gave her the strength to not give up on herself. It encouraged me tremendously!

Never did she *force* Jesus and/or the bible on me; she simply shared her truth, her story. She was a living testimony and it intrigued me to no end.

Just as in the word of God, the life of the Christ hating Saul was transformed into Apostle Paul, one of The Lord's most faithful servants, God can and will use anyone He chooses to do His work here on earth, regardless of their past, when they fully surrender to Him and His will for their life. That should be a huge encouragement to us all!

God knew just what I needed and who I needed to encourage me. I was always left asking myself, "Who is *this God?*" and "How has the way I've been living kept me from knowing Him in *this* way?"

There were many nights after our work was completed, that I would vent to Warkedia about my issues and struggles, and she would pull out devotionals and bible verses and we would both discuss and study them together. It helped me a great deal and I started looking forward to those times with expectation. One of the most essential things she did, which happened to be what a pretty forgetful girl like myself at the time needed, was that she constantly and consistently encouraged me to actually open my own bible at home and begin to read and study the Word *for myself* and to ask the *Holy Spirit* for the proper interpretation. It wasn't easy at first, because at the time I had a pattern of inconsistency, but I realized that the more I did what she encouraged me to do, the more I learned and had an eagerness to learn. My desire to understand The Word of God and The Creator of it became high on my priority list and not only that but I also began to feel a peace that I had never ever felt before. I didn't completely understand it all at once, but I knew for sure that 'whatever *this* was, it's what I needed!'

Not long after that, I moved on to a different job and no longer worked at the nursing home that we first met in, but Warkedia invited me to her church, which at the time was called New Wine Worship Center. The ministry was new to the area because Apostle Melvin Dickens and His wife, First Lady Sandra Dickens were originally from Maryland and had relocated to the city I resided in, York, Pennsylvania. The services were held in a very nice nearby hotel just minutes from my parents' home.

One of the very first things Apostle Melvin spoke over me, by way of the Holy Spirit, without knowing much, if anything about me personally at all, was, "You were at a place in your life where you were not ready to receive the Lord wholeheartedly. The Lord says… you're ready now." Soon after that, Apostle Melvin encouraged me to start *journaling,* again!

---

*Journaling has become my therapy and the very best way I can express myself, my thoughts, feelings, struggles, hopes and dreams. It has become another mighty way that I commune with my Heavenly Father. I remember my mother once told me during one of our many heart-to-hearts, that not only was she incredibly grateful to God for my growth in Him but also my love for writing and my desire and passion for journaling.*

*She said she felt as though it also helped save me, and I do agree!*

---

# PEACE

## PEACE
*Sunday, October 30th, 2011 @ 12am*

So, I was feeling so disheartened yesterday, just mixed feelings and emotions, loneliness and impatience. I was just down in my spirit because my circumstances aren't the best right now…. It's just a lonely time for me honestly, and I know I've come a long way, but this is another season I did not see coming. I assumed after the last season and chapter of my life nothing but sunshine would come, but God sure knows how to keep me humble! Yet, just as frustration was coming full force just now, I opened my devotional and it read:

"I want to warn you against setting your own watch. God's time is NOT your own".

Just those words alone reminded me that I need to get my mind and heart right and back in the proper perspective. Thank you, Jesus, for your peace, even during these difficult times.

**- KHAFA (Keeping Hope and Faith Alive)**

You know that saying that reads:
*"No God, No Peace. Know God, Know Peace?"*
That is a testimony in and of itself!
Most of my life, I knew *of* God.

My parents raised me in the admonition of the Lord, and we attended church and Sunday school every Sunday.

Throughout the years though, and through my own personal life experiences, I had come to realize that there is a distinct difference between truly knowing the Lord, and simply knowing *of* the Lord, as well as a distinct difference between being *religious,* and having a true and authentic *relationship* with your Heavenly Father.

I'm sure if you think hard enough, you can think of a number of people that you simply know of. Social media makes this easy to do because many of us tend to have hundreds and even thousands of "friends," and "followers," but how many of those people can we say that we really *know*? How many of them really *know* us?

Often, it's not too many. Now why is that?

Because it takes intimacy and time to learn the motives, characteristics, and personality traits of someone else in order to build a relationship with them to the point that we can confidently say that we truly *know* another human being.

It's no different with our Heavenly Father!

Most of the time that I spent only knowing *of* God, I also spent spinning my wheels, battling myself, not knowing whether to go left or right, emotionally unstable because I was heavily influenced by my surroundings and my circumstances, and just completely confused about both love and life as a whole!

When we find ourselves seeking peace and comfort in other things and other people, we open doors for added confusion as we watch ourselves and our lives spin even more out of control. Our need for peace and comfort is simply an indication that there is an area(s) in our lives where a void is present, a void that only our Heavenly Father, our Creator, can fill.

Impatience and loneliness are two things that will drive you into the direction and the arms of all the wrong things, opportunities and people, if not led by the Lord. Jesus wants to shower us with His peace that surpasses all understanding, if only we would rely on Him! At times He doesn't want us to do anything but *be still*. To simply be content (not complacent) with our circumstances, with the time and the season He has us in. Sometimes we want to run ahead of the Lord so much that we miss the opportunity for Him to show us what we need to learn in our current season, which will help equip and prepare us for the greater that is to come.

*"The Lord will fight for you, and you shall hold your peace and remain at rest."*
**Exodus 14:14 AMP**

The peace of God is incredibly powerful because through it, we receive His presence.

Far too often, when I wasn't seeking to fill a supposed void by way of something that could never truly satisfy a need, I found myself in a habit of constantly seeking the Lords *hand,* what I felt I needed, what I felt I lacked…and not seeking His face and His *heart!*

Seek His face, and there, His presence will surround you.

Get to truly know Him, for in His presence is where His peace resides!

*"And the peace of God [that peace which reassures the heart, that peace] which transcends all understanding [that peace which] stands guard over your hearts and your minds in Christ Jesus [is yours]."*
**Philippians 4:7 AMP**

Know GOD, Know PEACE.

## Question:

What areas in your life in which you have had a part to play in, that hindered the peace of God from overtaking your heart and your life?

_____

_____

_____

_____

_____

## *Prayer*

*Most Gracious God, thank you for your peace that surpasses all understanding! Lord, you are the ultimate comforter and I pray that as I draw nearer and nearer unto you, your Holy Spirit will both show me the root of my internal conflict and flood my heart with your peace that overpowers all uneasiness, anxiety, impatience and fear.*

*There is none like you. In Jesus mighty name I pray, Amen*

**JOY**

## JOY
*Wednesday Oct 4th, 2011 @ 2:00am*

Honestly, I feel like I have gotten so used to failure and disappointment that I can't even remember how it must feel to actually accomplish something and experience the feeling of consistently being happy.

Yet, the joy I feel this morning is indescribable! This really just goes to show that God is now in the driver seat [of my life], because I've finally let Him in and allowed Him to take over!

Lord, THANK YOU for taking the wheel and steering my life, I don't know how I ever thought of doing things without you! Never again. I'm getting to know you, for myself, and nobody can tell me ANYTHING [contrary]. Nothing has the power to separate me from you, Jesus.

Thank you for your mercy, faithfulness and patience. Not only do I really need it, I can sincerely say that absolutely no one compares to you.

**- KHAFA**

Happiness is an awesome feeling; it can have us feeling absolutely on top of the world! When we're around the people we love, meet a goal we have set for ourselves, or because we are simply able to do what we've been purposed to do—that, and many other things result in and add to our happiness.

But what about the times when those things are not occurring as we thought they would or should? What if, like Job in the Bible, all that we love and cherish is taken away from us without being given a reason or immediate answer as to why? What happens when temporary situations and circumstances don't allow us to be able to achieve our goals? What if we don't even know what our true purpose, passion or calling is, just yet?

The thing about that emotion called happiness, that we love so much, is that most of the time it is brought on by external circumstances that are typically working in our favor.

*In our favor.*

Yet, many are aware that all of life and its circumstances do not always *feel* as though they are working in our favor-- so then what?

I believe, this is where *joy,* more specifically, the *joy of the Lord,* plays a crucial part.

Have you ever been around a believer who had every 'right' to be down and out?

Perhaps their life, from the outside looking in, was in shambles. Maybe all the odds were stacked against them. Perhaps they had received bad news, or their health was at risk, yet their light and the light of God literary radiated from within, even through their storm.

*That* is an indication of the *joy of the Lord!*

*"The LORD is my strength and my [impenetrable] shield; My heart trusts [with unwavering confidence] in Him, and I am helped; Therefore my heart greatly rejoices, And with my song I shall thank Him and praise Him."*
**Psalms 28:7 AMP**

The Holy Spirit resides within all of us who truly believe, therefore, joy is indeed an *inside job.*

It's about being realistic about our current situation, but being able to look beyond it. Being confident that because we know who holds our life in the palm of His hands and because He sees all things and knows all things, where many may sulk and lose hope, we are still able to hold our head up and smile from within because we know that our God is both constantly and diligently working behind the scenes on our behalf! That knowledge gives us hope, even through our trials. It's where our strength derives from.

The joy of the Lord is our strength and as a child of God, under His covering, we are blessed to receive both!

In 2009 I was clinically diagnosed with situational depression and anxiety. The amazing thing, next to the fact that the Lord stepped in right in the nick of time in my life, was the fact that the feelings I felt and the things I was experiencing were all *situational.* Because I allowed myself to be totally and completely consumed by the negativity and the confusion, in which God is not the author of (1 Corinthians 14:33), the effect of the heartbreak and the disappointment that I was feeling progressed and had a way of taking me over.

One thing I have learned throughout the years is that by the grace of God, every single storm we face in life does have an end-date.

In time, *it will seize!*

*"They who sow in tears shall reap with joyful singing."*
**Psalms 126:5 AMP**

Life is not always easy; things and situations will not always go the way we desire for them to. With this knowledge, we must choose how we will weather the storms of life. There's something so indescribable about the joy of the Lord. As we draw nearer to Him, we will stand in awe at how His presence and the security that His Word brings to our hearts literally sets us up for victory over practically any storm we face!

*I have told these things so that my joy and delight may be in you and that your joy may be made full and complete and overflowing.*
**John 15:11 AMP**

## Question:

What outside forces (people, places, habits etc.) do you believe you have used, either now or in your past, that have resulted in happiness that only lasted temporarily?

_____

_____

_____

_____

_____

## *Prayer*

*Lord God, thank you, for I declare that your joy is indeed my strength! It gives me the ability to push through and weather the storms that I'm faced with, for I know that you are right here with me; I am never facing them alone. May I forever seek refuge in you and not in any distractions that are designed to bring me temporary happiness and/or ultimately take me off course. May your light radiate in and through me as I claim victory through Jesus Christ.*

*I choose joy, I choose you. In Jesus mighty name I pray, Amen*

# IDENTITY

### IDENTITY
*September 18th, 2017 @ 1:25pm*

I may have not yet had a significant other who has been able to stick/stand by my side through all of the sunshine and the storms, but God has blessed me thus far immensely with loved ones, both family and friends that by love, have become family, who have. Yet and still, all that I've had to overcome, God has had me going through it with only one 24/7 consistent person by my side...**Him.**

Lol, He did that on purpose. He has to ensure that I know exactly who He is, and the role He must always play in my life. It's been vital, and in spite of all the tears that were shed prior to that, it was well worth it and will forever be!

I cannot do, think, or become anything, if He is not leading me. I never want to. I will never be able to.

**- KHAFA**

The Merriam- Webster dictionary definition of *identity* as it pertains to individuality is: "The distinguishing character or personality of an individual."[1]

I can't help but think back to when the concept of an intimate relationship with Jesus Christ was so utterly foreign to me. The person I thought I was back then and who I know I am in Christ now, differs, greatly!

From my perception and perspective on things, to how I chose to deal with my obstacles and roadblocks, it all differed tremendously. As I continue to grow, I trust that years from now I will also look back on these current days and see how much further I've come, by God's grace.

Our walk with Christ is a *life-long journey*. No matter where we stand or how long we've been saved, we can trust that *He isn't done with us yet* and just when we think we know a great deal, He finds a way to remind us that we still have so much more to learn!

Come to think of it, I had not the slightest idea of who I really was, nor did I ever really stop to figure *me* out! I was simply coasting through life, going with the flow, crossing my fingers and hoping that along the way I would somehow piece myself together.

Sad, but true.

If we know within our hearts that we are a creation, formed in our mother's womb by The Creator, The Almighty God, why would we bother going through this journey called life, and not seek *Him* for our *true* identity. In doing so we prevent ourselves from going through life with the probability of finding out in the end that we may have not only been living a lie, but that He may have also had so much more in store that we never allowed

---

1       Identity. (n.d) In Merriam-Webster's collegiate dictionary. Retrieved from http://www.merriam-webster.com/dictionary/identity

ourselves to experience.

Some may believe that we just *happen to somehow* find ourselves, over time.

I have sat and watched as years passed by, and many of my peers and I seemed to have either unintentionally or purposely chosen to go *with the flow*. Like ships without sails, with no *true* direction, learning about ourselves but never truly *finding* ourselves.

*Our identity is rooted and grounded in the eternal being that created and saved us.*

*Our true identity is found in Jesus Christ.*

But until we realize and recognize this, the world and all of its many influences will shape our identity for us, leaving us no other option but to believe that the person we have somehow become, is who we are and all that we will ever be.

> *"Yet you, LORD, are our Father; we are the clay, and You our potter, and we all are the work of your hand."*
> **Isaiah 64:8 AMP**

To be molded more and more into *His* likeness. *That* is the ultimate goal.

As we travel through life, we grow to realize that in every season, with every passing day, there a multitude of facts and realizations that we come to learn about ourselves. We are faced with the understanding that in order to allow true growth to take place in our lives, we must also *un-learn* some things; more things than we may initially want to admit.

See, one of the beauties of being a child of the Most High God, is the constant state of reconstruction, rebuilding and purging that He keeps us in. Our God is not mediocre, He is not surface, nor will He allow His children to be. Yes, it can be much easier to simply deal with things on the surface, but I have learned, and at times the hard way, that our Heavenly Father really does not get down like that!

The Lord intends to get down to the root; the root of our problems, our frustrations, our weaknesses and He then he elevates us from within. He does so from the inside, out.

*"And the risk it took to remain tight in a bud was more painful than the risk it took to bloom"* - **Anais Nin**

In 2011, I heard that quote as the intro of an Alicia Keys album entitled, "The Element of Freedom" that happened to be one of my favorites at the time. I distinctly remember thinking, "This is *exactly* how I feel, *but about The Lord* and my journey in Him! Lord, I can't stay here anymore; I have to bloom in order to be free in **You!**"

*I was desperate for change; the kind of change only God can create.*

I became so tired of being lost. I may not have looked lost on the outside but I was feeling completely off course from within. As I was led more and more by the Holy Spirit it quickly became apparent to me that my true identity was emerging. The closer I drew to the Lord and the deeper I went in Him, and the more I let go of the fight to do everything my way, the more I started becoming molded into the likeness of God.

But let me tell you, this was (and still is) a *process...*

## *Purging*

To fully discover all that we truly are, we must also realize and recognize what we are not.

Once we know the truth of whom we are and who we are destined by God to be, we will be able to quickly identify everything that is contrary to that.

This may include the lies we were told about ourselves by others and/or the lies we have repeatedly spoken over our own lives; as well as the characteristics and behaviors that we have acquired over time that we have failed to denounce that have now resulted in us taking on an identity that is not who we are destined to be.

You know those excuses that so many of us may have either used or heard:

*"That's just me/who I am"* or *"You can't teach an old dog new tricks?"*

They simply result from stubbornness and an unwillingness to change, because the fact that we *can* change, is undeniable.

**2 Corinthians 5:17** destroys the notion that we cannot change:

> *"Therefore, if anyone is in Christ, He is a new creation. The old has passed away; behold, the new has come!"*

We were destined to evolve; destined to cast away our old ways and become *new in Christ*.

*It begins with the heart.*

When the heart is willing to change, willing to face and embrace even the unpleasant truths of our current realities in order to set our true identities back on course, we recognize that the Lord has been patiently waiting for us all along!

*There is no human being walking this earth that has the immeasurable, inexhaustible patience of The Lord Jesus Christ.*

When we are ready to repent and surrender to the Lord, He goes to work on our behalf!

It is important to include in our prayers to the Lord, a request that He fill us with the very same characteristics that identify Him, such as, love, patience, holiness, faithfulness, and honesty, amongst many others. It is also vital that we ask God to reveal and remove all of the things within us that are unlike Him. The things that ultimately keep us from walking in righteousness and hinder us from seeing ourselves as Christ sees us!

## *Inadequacy*

I battled with the spirit of inadequacy for years. It's a tough battle that constantly lingers and one that the enemy uses to keep us bound to mediocrity and worthlessness. It's also one, if not dealt with, that we can use over time as an excuse to refrain from pursuing greatness.

It's one that only God can fight on our behalf, but it requires us to know our worth and to speak *life* to ourselves and over ourselves.

At times it's as if all Satan needs is a crack in our lives and our spirits to let his destructive spirit freely enter.

The crack that the enemy used with me was created by heartbreak.

It is vital to sit and allow the Lord to reveal to us the *root* of our issues regardless if they unfortunately cause us to remember places and situations that we would rather not go back to or deal with.

I learned from my own experience, that allowing the Lord to take us to this place is not only needed, but it is necessary and truly worth it in the end!

I was blessed to have been raised in an extremely loving and supportive God-fearing family, but that didn't keep me from having my own hurdles to overcome. I always say that every hill and valley in our life, are ultimate blessings because there is always something to either rejoice over, or learn from. God does not waste any opportunity for growth!

I experienced love for the first time in my late teens/early 20's, as well as what it meant to love selflessly, though not necessarily *properly* (in the eyesight of God).

Coming from a place where my confidence as a teenager, turned young adult, was admittedly not the best, the effects of experiencing the loss of that love took me on an emotional whirlwind and I was quickly faced with the constant battle of "am I good enough?". "Why am I not good enough?", "If someone I care for **this** much and feel I have given all I possibly could to no longer sees my worth, then am I even worthy!?"

We fall into a terrible trap of feeling less than and feeling inadequate when we begin to seek validation from outside sources and don't receive it the way we were intended to. I learned this lesson the hard way but as I look back, I also came to realize that where pain resided is also where in time, gratefulness began to overflow.

The trials and the tribulations that the Lord allows us to experience are really for our own good and if we develop the proper perspective through the process, we not only *go* through those trials, we also *grow* through them and come out winning!

Believe it or not, in certain situations we learn to be grateful for the consequences of our actions.

*One of the biggest lessons the Lord was teaching me from and* *through the heartbreak I was experiencing, was the importance of being mindful not to desire any of God's creations **more** than I desire The Creator.*

This took me years to realize though; 6 long years to be exact. The lesson wasn't solely about love, itself, as it was about first taking me back to developing a true relationship with *The Source* of love, my Heavenly Father. I would never learn how to *properly* love, in a way that God is pleased with and until I understood this concept, He is the center of it all!

In order to do so, I had to first learn my true identity by seeing myself through the eyes of Christ.

**Question:**

What behavior, habit or character trait can you admit was or still is difficult to change even though you know that in one way or another, it isn't pleasing to God?

_____

_____

_____

_____

_____

**\*Prayer\***

*Thank you, Heavenly Father, for my true identity which is found in nothing and no one but you. Help me to be able to see myself the way you see me; through your eyes, Lord. My worth and my value comes from you. I come against all tactics of the enemy to convince me not only of what and who I am not, but to also persuade me that I cannot be molded into your likeness. May I learn to forever speak life and your Word over myself and my circumstances as I continue on this journey of self-discovery and confidence that is found in you.*

*In Jesus mighty name I pray, Amen*

# ADVICE/CORRECTION

## ADVICE/ CORRECTION
*November 15th, 2011 @ 11:05pm*

Whew! It sure is important to know the Lord and His Word because He definitely put me in check today! But see, what I love about God's correction is that I don't feel condemned, I just feel a strong conviction and an urge to change! I really never knew I could be as grateful for His correction as I would typically be for His many blessings. Wow, that's how you know your love for the Lord is growing! The Word of God says only fools despise His corrections. I feel like taking an even more in-depth inventory of my entire life and asking Him to show me every single place that I'm falling short and can improve, so I can start doing so! It really is true that the Lord loves us just the way we are, but He loves us way too much to leave us the way He found us.

I don't feel any better or accepting of what I've done wrong, if anything I'm sincerely encouraged to seriously ***get it together*** because this really is no joke and I really am set-apart. I have to live it.

I went about many things the wrong way in the past. I am both grateful and anxious for the opportunity to do things the right way going forward, as God leads me.

**- KHAFA**

It's no fun for many to be told when they're wrong, and then accepting that they have done something improperly or have gone about things the wrong way. In fact, the issue of pride has resulted in many people being reluctant to accept any form of correction from others. If this applies to us in any way, all that this does is hold us back from the growth that's needed in becoming the men and women God has created us to be.

When a parent corrects their child, typically, it's because they do not want their child to continue making the same mistakes that result in consequences that could easily be avoided. With God being Our Heavenly Father, that is a major reason for His correction towards us.

*Love is also displayed through heartfelt correction.*

The Lord is the creator of this entire universe, and the creator of our lives, He knows the beginning from the end of all things.

If you knew of someone who was aware of the end results for decisions that you were contemplating on, or actions you were already actively engaging in, wouldn't you be inclined to take heed to their advice?

God's Word is so beautifully and purposely filled with instruction and advice for how He desires His children to live on this earth as we evolve into who He has destined for us to become. It lays out for us how His desire is for us to grow more and more into His likeness as we share His word and His love everywhere that we go and everywhere we are planted.

As I've seen it both written and spoken before:

*B*asic
*I*nstructions

**B**efore
**L**eaving
**E**arth

My experience and growth in Christ, thus far, has literally been life changing and it's as if the Lord knew just how I would react to certain situations, and also how stuck in my ways I could be before I wholeheartedly opened my heart up to Him so that he could work on me and in me.

I have made a ton of mistakes in my 32 years of life thus far! Thank God for His saving grace! I can say though without a shadow of a doubt, that I have personally never felt *condemned* by my Heavenly Father!

Growing up, my brother and I were always in church. We attended Sunday school, vacation bible school and my family often had weekly family devotions as well. My parents laid such an amazing foundation, but it's true that the true test of faith arises when we are faced with our own personal challenges. The pain from those challenges and the un-willingness to take the time to understand God's purpose for allowing them, sent me on a journey of trying to find some form of peace for my pain. I completely overlooked the fact that true and total peace is and can only ever be found in the Lord.

See, when you don't seek God for your comfort and healing, you will very easily find things that will *temporarily* help fill the voids, but ultimately, they will take you off the course that God has for you.

God gave me, as he does each one of us, *free will*.

With that free will, I chose to turn to things that temporarily took away my loneliness. I turned to drinking and fornicating to keep me from thinking about all that I was going through on the inside. I allowed myself to become involved with people that I didn't have a purposeful commitment to.

Now, I know many people would say "what's the big deal, that's the 'norm' for many". But just because something is normal to the world, does not mean it is at all, approved by God.

*"And do not conform to this world [any longer with its superficial values and customs], but be transformed and progressively changed [as you mature spiritually] by the renewing of your mind [focusing on godly values and ethical attitudes], so that you may prove [for yourselves] what the will of God is, that which is good and acceptable and perfect [in His plan and purpose for you]."*
**Romans 12:2 AMP**

Not only that, but in the process of it all, my actions and some of my constant and consistent associations clouded my mind and my judgment, as well as my own personal worth and value that I was raised to be aware of all my life.

Still, even after realizing I had nowhere else to go and nowhere else to look, but *up,* certain things just didn't quite seem like a big deal.

The Lord knew this, and before He began the process of the much-needed correction and redirection I needed, He showered me with *love;* His true and unconditional love, *Agape love.*

The type of love that draws you in, wraps you in its arms *just as you are* and reminds you that you have never strayed too far, or made a mistake too big to be forgiven, to turn back to Him, and to begin again.

*Righteousness* is something I never understood before I began to develop my own personal relationship with the Lord because I never bothered to take the time to understand it. I admittingly viewed *holiness* as just a prideful, stuck up behavior and mentality that I wanted no part of. I felt like such acts would never be natural to me. I couldn't see how "God" was a part of that, because I believe deep down, I mistakenly viewed it as a negative thing. In time though, I learned that righteousness is in fact not by our *works,* but by our *faith* in God and I learned this through my growth in Christ.

It's His loving kindness towards me as I got to know Him more and more for myself that also drew Him closer to me. As this occurred, and I got to know and honor Him for who He truly is, the more my heart started to develop a *desire* to live a life that this God who loves me so much and has been there for me all along, would be pleased with. It is then that He began the gradual process, not through condemnation, but by way of conviction, of opening my heart to receive His correction.

*The closer I got to the Lord, the more I experienced true conviction and the conviction increased my desire to walk in righteousness.*

That desire that I began to develop redirected me and led me to spiritual conviction where the Holy Spirit began to show me my sins, the way I was living and the things I was doing that were not pleasing to the God that I served, the God that had plans to prosper me and not to harm me. My actions that could have resulted in me harming myself, and the carelessness of placing myself in positions where I could be harmed by others became more and more evident to me. Some of the things that at one point didn't bother me at all, started to make me feel uncomfortable and undeniably uneasy.

That was and is nothing but the power of God, the power of the

Holy Spirit at work within me.

This led me to *repentance*. Acknowledging what I knew in my heart and according to the Word of God that's not right, asking Him for His forgiveness, thanking Him for His grace, and striving to change my ways.

> "*So repent [change your inner self—your old way of thinking, regret past sins] and return [to God—seek His purpose for your life], so that your sins may be wiped away [blotted out, completely erased], so that times of refreshing may come from the presence of the Lord. [restoring you like a cool wind on a hot day]*"
> **Acts 3:19 AMP**

As Maya Angelou once stated, "…when you *know* better, you *do* better."

In *John 8:11*, after Jesus stands up for and protects the adulterous woman from being stoned, reminding the Scribes and Pharisees that neither of them are without sin, He then turns to the woman and states "..Then neither do I condemn you", and He follows that statement by giving her an instruction, in love: "Now go, and sin no more".

As a child of God, this is an instruction for each one of us and should serve as a continuous reminder to strive not to repeat the same mistakes while we allow God to help us make better and wiser choices that will result in better outcomes.

The outcomes that He has planned for us all along!

## Question:

How has correction and/or conviction from the Lord, in time, ever helped to improve your results in something you were pursuing or a particular area or season of your life as a whole?

_____

_____

_____

_____

_____

## *Prayer*

*Heavenly Father, thank you for your divine correction and conviction; for I know that it is a true demonstration of your endless love for me. Give me the strength to continually walk in obedience, walking in your ways, steering clear of all that is harmful to me and doesn't represent you.*

*I know that it is ultimately all for my good and for your Glory. In Jesus mighty name, Amen.*

# WORTH/HEALING

## WORTH/ HEALING
*January 1st, 2018 @ 8:45am*

It's a new day. A new year!

To God be the glory! 2017 was a blessed year for me and through it all, God showed Himself incredibly faithful in my life!

Now, the most sincere desire of my heart has yet to be fulfilled but God is surely moving in the direction and areas of my life the way *He* chooses, therefore I surrender to Him and I believe that in the year 2018 many things will grow and expand. My steps with be ordered even more by the grace of God!

2017 may have ended in a disappointing way as it pertains to the desires of my heart, but thank God my hope is not in man, but in God! I know He has no plan to play me, and He in fact has plans to prosper me, according to His Word. Therefore, what I need to do for myself is let out these tears of disappointment [which I've learned not to keep bottled up inside], spend more quality time with my Heavenly Father, and *keep it moving!*

Because trust me, I *will* keep moving! This new-year is about to be amazing by the grace of God, nothing will hold me back and everything will come together, the right way, at the right time!

**- KHAFA**

There are times when things have a way of quickly taking place, changing and suddenly you experiencing a divine turnaround practically overnight. The power of God is limitless, and these things are absolutely possible if and when God wills it. There are times when God purposely and strategically moves, suddenly, *just like that!*

A majority of the time though, that didn't happen to be the case for me.

Thankfully I knew that I wasn't operating by "luck"; I was operating by the grace of my Heavenly Father and had faith that He would see me through.

*Heartbreak is huge.*

Depending on your age, your maturity level, or simply the level of pain that heartbreak brings you, this type of disappointment can have you so confused that you don't know where to turn to, where to go or who and what to lean on. Being *that* broken has a way of making you realize that trying to piece yourself back together *on your own* is doing you way more harm than good.

It was also that level of pain though that I feel helped thrust me into my destiny!

In time, many believers begin to actually understand why it is said that in order for God to truly use His children, the process of being rebuilt *by Him* after being broken in one way or another throughout their lives must take place.

In order for God to truly use us for greatness and for His glory, we must learn to *surrender;* it's a prerequisite.

I have a feeling that the Lord knew I was a bit too *hard-headed* to ever fully surrender if I didn't first find myself in a place where there was nowhere else for me to look to, but up to Him.

*"Broken things can become blessed things when you let God do the mending."*
**- Author Unknown**

I can attest to the accuracy of this quote because my own personal experiences taught me the truth in it. I can say that if I hadn't been broken the way I was; if my heart hadn't been shattered and the direction I began to walk in hadn't been the opposite direction of where the Lord had a desire for me to go and grow, I'm not sure that I would have ever been in the proper position to be ready and willing to be used by God. I would've thought that I had it all together and probably wouldn't have understood the vitality of keeping God at the center of *all* things.

This is where many of our testimonies are birthed from…our tests!

Before God was ever able to begin strategically using me the way He saw fit, for His glory, there was a great deal of healing that had to take place and this healing was a continual process. I can transparently say that my original mindset was that because I had chosen Jesus and now desired to live for Him, that my pain would be cast out just as *quickly* and as far out as His Word says my sins were cast away from me:

*"As far as the east is from the west, so far has He removed our transgressions from us."*
**Psalms 103:12 AMP**

Yes, in time, true and total healing does and did occur!

But my internal pain and emotions were not healed quite as fast as I had anticipated.

*Over time,* I fully came to the realization that this was indeed a process that I also had a large part to play in all along!

I needed to learn to speak *life* to myself, just as **Proverbs 18:21** states:

*Life and death are in the power of the tongue and those who love it will reap its fruits.*

I needed to constantly remind myself of God's word, His promises over my life, His healing power and the fact that He is in complete control. It had become evident that just as I desired healing, Satan and his agents were working to keep me in bondage, bound and broken.

I learned that this is to be expected. The last thing the enemy wants is to see any one of God's children rise in Christ, become born again, step out of the darkness and into Gods marvelous light and allow themselves and their hearts to be opened to and transformed by the Lord. When this occurs, we are able to fully receive Christ, be led by the Holy Spirit and allow God to use us to share the love of Christ and the truth of God's Word in order to advance His Kingdom for His glory!

Know, that this is the total opposite of Satan's agenda and therefore *he will fight. The attack is real,* but in the end he will lose every single time, for He has already lost!

*As the bride of Christ, we are victorious!*

My broken state sure was a trying process but by the grace of God it didn't last forever!

God used every wounded and crushed part of me that He mended as an example of His saving grace, to show that He is the *ultimate healer.*

He took my crushed confidence and showed me that I had begun seeking validation in areas that could never sustain me and He began to rebuild my confidence, *in Him,* on a sturdy foundation so that no matter the circumstance, rejection would never again make me question my worth and my value.

The intriguing thing about the Lord is that at times He will use a situation to teach us a lesson, but He wouldn't be God unless He *tests* us as well. The lives we live consist of hills and valleys, so when situations occur we have to be able to stand strong and tall in the Lord in the midst of adversity. I came to realize that the tests are not to harm us but to ensure that we have fully grasped and learned the lessons from within.

*As I passed the tests moving forward, I then realized that I had experienced true healing from within.*

Only God can do that!

Question:

What situation did you encounter, whether emotional, physical or spiritual, that at some point you felt as though you would never heal from?

_____

_____

_____

_____

_____

How has your healing from it changed your perspective moving forward?

_____

_____

_____

_____

_____

## *Prayer*

*Most Gracious God, thank you for creating me in your image, for even when life's circumstances attempt to dismay and discourage me, I am reminded of my worth and that just as your Word states, I am clothed with strength and dignity! By the authority vested in me through Jesus Christ, may I continually and confidentially speak life to myself and my circumstances, standing firm on the knowledge that you are the God of healing.*

*What is impossible with man, is most certainly possible with God.*

*In Jesus mighty name I pray, Amen*

# PURPOSE

## PURPOSE
*February 10th, 2018 @ 10am*

### Dream

There was a gathering at one of my family members' homes. We were being loud and happened to disturb one of the neighbors. She was a young girl and we got into a little confrontation with her at her door for some reason. She got very defensive and ended up slamming the door in our faces. We all went back to our family members home and proceeded with our celebration. In my heart I felt bad about how the situation had went, so I began to write her a letter. I had planned to slip the letter under her door, when all of a sudden, she barged into my family members home. When she came straight up the steps, the first person she recognized was me. She tapped me on the shoulder and asked to speak to me outside. It just so happened that we both felt bad about what went down and explained and apologized to one another about the encounter we all recently had. I ended up sharing the Love of Christ with her and I remember it being an awesome discussion!

Not too long after we departed, I saw an ambulance arriving at her home and she was rushed to the hospital. I did not know if she ended up passing away or what had occurred, but I remember in the end, I was overwhelmed with gratitude to God that she and I were able to have that discussion about the Word of God and the Love of Christ!

\*\*\* All I know is that if anything, the dream confirms to me that throughout my life God will put me in positions, at times that may seem random and maybe even initially uncomfortable, but they are in fact strategic and purposeful. They will be opportunities for me to share His love, His Word, and His light with others. You never know what others are going through or what is to come in their lives. Absolutely everyone needs Him.

He will use me as a vessel in many ways and I simply need to be obedient when convicted and led by The Holy Spirit!

Thank you for choosing me, Daddy. Shine your light, order my steps, direct my path, give me strength and speak through me, Lord!

**- KHAFA**

Purpose is a word that I was taught the importance of growing up, but I didn't fully grasp the *weight* of it until I began to see myself the way my Creator sees me.

It wasn't until I began to draw nearer to the Lord and learning for myself just how great and mighty *He* is, that I stopped and asked myself, "Why me?".

Why did a being so great and mighty *create me?* Why did Jesus *save me?* Why did He *choose me?*

*Like, really ... Why?*

> *"For I know the plans and thoughts that I have for you, says the LORD, plans for peace and well-being and not for disaster, to give you a future and a hope."*
> **Jeremiah 29:11 AMP**

*If God has plans for me, and has a purposeful future for me, how do I ensure that I'm lined up with it? How do I even know if I'm headed in the right direction?*

Once we begin to understand that we didn't just "happen", but that we are created by God for a *reason,* we become convicted and anxious to find out what that reason is!

I began to understand that this reason is my ultimate purpose.

> *"Before I formed you in your mother's womb, I knew you [and approved of you as my chosen instrument], and before you were born I consecrated you [to Myself as My own]; I have appointed you as a prophet to the nations."*
> **Jeremiah 1:5 AMP**

I came to realize that as children of God, what He has called each and every one of us to do is to love Him, others, and to share His truth and the saving grace of Jesus Christ with the world. Sharing the good news, the love of Christ and winning souls for the Kingdom of God by allowing others to not only hear about God from us but to see God in us, is our ultimate purpose.

*The ultimate reason we are here, is to bring glory to God in all that we do.*

It puts the things we strive to do in proper perspective when we seek God as to whether what we choose to pursue is simply and solely of our own will and desire, or in line with His will for our lives.

One of the most amazing things that I've truly grasped, just within the last few years, is the mere fact that God can and will use His children, in any way that *He* sees fit, to bring Him glory! It doesn't have to look any particular way, or be the same way He has done it in and through others.

No two individuals walking this earth are identical. We all have our own individual make up, our own distinct and purposefully God-given design. Therefore, *how* He chooses for us to live out our life's ultimate purpose of bringing glory to His name, will also differ! He has given us His Holy Word as instruction, and formed us all with our own gifts, talents, abilities and interests. He makes no mistakes and desires to work in us to ensure that we grow in all that He's placed within us so that we can make a mark on this world for His glory.

*Our uniqueness in God will be a determining factor in the uniqueness of how we carry out our purpose.*

I remember I use to think that you were never really "living for God" if your career or title was not a Preacher, Bishop, Deacon, Apostle, Minister, Evangelist or any other ministry leader.

*How ignorant, right?*

Now, if one does come to the realization that God has placed such an incredible and powerful calling on their life, it is surely not one to take lightly or for granted. There are great and mighty things He plans to do in and through an individual with such an anointing!

But if Christ truly lives within us, wherever we go and in all that we do, He should be represented. There is absolutely no limit to all that He can and will do through each and every one of us. I've seen and also been used by God in some of the most unexpected, most unconventional ways and places. I believe the Lord loves to *show up and show out* in order to remind us that absolutely nothing is impossible with Him!

> *"But Jesus looked at them and said, 'With man [as far as it depends on them] it is impossible, but with God all things are possible.'"*
> **Matthew 19:26 AMP**

Regardless of whether God has called us to ministry or to be school teachers, lawyers, IT professionals, producers, engineers, healthcare professionals, police officers, case managers or any and everything in between, if our hearts are open and we allow the Holy spirit to lead us, God can and will use us mightily. God can use us right where we are at and wherever He takes us; to show His love and spread His truth. Although God is a god of order, things don't have to be done a typical or traditional way or have a particular setup in order for God to move. He can and will show Himself strong and use us to reach the lost in any way He sees fit and deems necessary.

---

## Why do I need to be SAVED and what does that have to do with my life and the purpose I pursue?

---

When I was away at college, "on my own", I typically only opened my bible when something was going wrong. I felt, at least in that moment, that I needed help from a source greater than myself. I knew the "basics" of Christianity, that Jesus Christ died for my sins on the cross at Calvary.

I knew this, but I didn't have the most thorough understanding of it. We can be told and taught everything that happened leading up to the death of Our Savior, and after, but it will tend to hold very little weight and importance to us in the grand scheme of things if we don't take the time to *understand* it for ourselves and how it affects us as we live out our lives. Through this, I also realized that my parents did their part to raise me, my brother and all those who lived with us, from time to time, in the discipline and admonition of the Lord to the very best of their ability. They played their part, did their duties and they did it well. Yet and still, we cannot be saved through or because of our connection with our parents, or any other individual.

Our relationship with The Lord is in fact a personal, 1-on-1 bond.

When I began to embark on my own journey with Christ is when I began to hear people talking about when they were *"saved."* To be honest, prior to that season of my life, I had ignorantly assumed that every person was already saved; that it was a done deal for us all once Christ died on the cross, whether we chose to acknowledge or accept Him or not. My thought (which I often kept to myself) was:

"Uh, wasn't I saved at birth or at my Christening?!"

It wasn't until I went through my own process of rededicating my life to Christ by surrendering my *entire* life to Him, that it began to make sense to me.

Up until that point, I never even knew I needed *saving*, because that would've insinuated that I was somehow *lost* or *in danger*. My own personal struggles allowed me to understand that as blessed as I was, solely by the grace of God, something in and about my life was just not right. I came to realize that not only was I lost, living a life that God wasn't the center of, that I didn't allow Him to lead or seek His perfect guidance in, but yes, I also was in fact in danger. In the end, nothing good would come from living a life that the Creator of not just our own lives, but also of the entire world, is not pleased with.

*"Only one life, 'twill soon be past, only what's done for Christ will last..."*
**- C.T Studd**

God wasn't the head of my life, so I would've continued making mistakes and decisions that surely would've led me down dead-end roads and even more dangerous consequences.

Thank God for both His grace and His mercy!

He reached into my darkness and pulled me into His marvelous light!

---

## OK. So I'm saved, now what?

---

When the Lord arrested my heart, filled me with His love and began to bless me with more and more understanding of His Word as well as His plan and desire for me, my entire perspective began to change in the most positive way.

When God is the head of our lives and the center of all that we do, we know that though trials will still present themselves, we can never go wrong in the end. When we have that understanding engraved in our hearts and minds, we are given the ability to boldly and confidently walk in our purpose, just as our Heavenly Father intends for us to do. We can use our gifts and talents to bring glory to His name. Not only are we not doing it alone, we are actually being *led* by the Holy Spirit that now dwells within us. As we continue to lean more and more on the Lord for instruction and direction, the more He leans towards us and provides us with all that we need.

*The more we yield, the more we will receive.*

This may not necessarily be the case for everyone, but one thing that became very apparent to me over time is that when I looked at my past, and even my present, anytime I was moving forth trying to accomplish things that I had never sincerely sought God for, more times than not, they crumbled and fell through, right before my very eyes. This wasn't because I was a "bad person" or that I was necessarily being "punished" (which at times I started to believe, solely out of pure frustration) but because:

1.  I was most likely heading down a path that may not have

been a "bad choice", necessarily, but was not at all God's will and desire for my life and may have also been a way of God's divine protection.

and/or

2. God *needed* me to fully grasp the understanding that *apart from Him, I can do nothing!*

*"I am the Vine; you are the branches. The one who remains in Me and I in him bears much fruit, for [otherwise] apart from Me [that is, cut off from vital union with Me] you can do nothing."*
**John 15:5 AMP**

My confidence, which was almost completely lost in the world, but found again in the God who created me, gave and continues to give me the assurance I need to know that if the Lord Himself has led me, to use what He has given me to fulfill the ultimate purpose He has for me here on earth, then He will also see me all the way through it, for His glory.

The Lord, having an ultimate purpose for us, gives us all the needed strength, motivation and zeal to press on, knowing that He has brought us way too far, to leave us now!!

**Question:**

Have you ever felt as though you didn't have a purpose, or that what you were pursuing wasn't aligned with the will of God for your life?

_____

_____

_____

_____

_____

If you are at that point, how are you now assured/ how has it been confirmed that you are now walking in the purpose of God for your life?

_____

_____

_____

_____

_____

**\*Prayer\***

*Heavenly Father, thank you for creating me with a plan and purpose and ensuring that through your Word, I am reminded that not only are you with me every step of the way, but that you have also already gone ahead of me. You know my future as well, without a doubt and have plans for me to ultimately succeed, plans to prosper me and not to harm me.*

*In you I have hope, and as you order my steps that lead to greatness, you alone will be glorified.*

*In Jesus mighty name I pray, Amen.*

# STRENGTH

## STRENGTH
*February 13th, 2017 @ 10am*

I thank the Holy Spirit for helping me combat the solemn state that wants to overtake me during this season. Today I was reminded once again of Jesus' message to doubting Thomas "Because you have seen me, you have believed; blessed are those who have not seen and yet believe" (John 20:29) and this is what I feel as though the Holy Spirit wants me to gather from that right now:

"You are not an **outcast,** Jozelle (Luopu), you are **set apart!**"

Yes, God has and is blessing many around me in various ways which is in turn drawing them nearer to Him. To God be the glory for that! God can work in so many ways and use whatever is needed to draw us nearer to Him. The point is not when we recognize His love and draw near, it's that we finally do draw near with a sincere heart!

But then it also came over me, "Blessed are you, Luopu (Jozelle), who has not yet seen...yet you still believe! Great is your portion!"

It's one great thing to believe God after He has done a great thing, and it's another thing to simply stand on faith alone, believing and declaring what He said, without yet seeing a thing. They all in the end represent the power of faith; but it takes a special kind of faith and strength when you choose to believe God for what neither you nor anyone else has yet to see manifest in your life. To others, you may look a little crazy, extra, lacking, or even desperate. But to the Lord, you are simply walking in His ways, walking in obedience and exercising your faith on an even greater level. I believe He will honor this.

God will do it and He alone will be glorified for it!

Thank you Lord for using me as an example. Thank you for

making my up-coming story a beautiful testimony. Thank you for setting me apart and for giving me the strength needed to be who you have called me to be and to wait on your promises. The journey has not been easy—not one bit. But I know that by the grace of the one true and living God that I serve, it will be undoubtedly worth it, In Jesus Name!

**- KHAFA**

Can you imagine what it must be like to watch those you not only love, but *created*, scramble as they strive to work and piece together this thing called "life", in their *own* strength, *excluding* you, when you already know that the end result will be an epic fail? For a human, being a witness to such a process would lead to frustration, and possibly even lead to anger, for some.

The awesome thing about the Lord is that, though He knows that He is our anchor, our rock and our strong tower, as my fellow native Liberians would say, "He can give us *long rope*" basically meaning, He is very patient with us; He tends to give us chance after chance to get it right!

Thank God for His patience, His mercy and His heavy hand of grace that is truly sufficient!

Having the personality that I tend to exude, which I believe I probably inherited directly from my mother (ha-ha), it always seemed to be a natural instinct of mine to simply and automatically take on, tackle, and work through everything on my own. It was hardly ever an act I gave much thought to. To be honest, to a certain point, having an often quieter personality when I was much younger (depending on who I was around), but still exhibiting a go-getter mentality towards things that I wanted and/or was passionate about helped to carry me a good distance and helped me accomplish a number of things, big and small.

Yet and still, the fact will always and forever remain that our God is a jealous God, and in fact, having or developing the mindset in which we find ourselves solely depending on our own strength, as if we are the ultimate source of it all, is not at all pleasing to Him and is in fact dishonoring to our Lord.

*"But He has said to me, "My grace is sufficient for you [My loving kindness and My mercy are more than enough—always available—regardless of the situation]; for [My] power is being perfected [and is completed and shows itself most effectively] in [your] weakness."Therefore, I will all the more gladly boast in my weaknesses, so that the power of Christ [may completely enfold me and] may dwell in me. 10 So I am well pleased with weaknesses, with insults, with distresses, with persecutions, and with difficulties, for the sake of Christ; for when I am weak [in human strength], then I am strong [truly able, truly powerful, truly drawing from God's strength]."*
**2 Corinthians 12:9-10 AMP**

The Lord has shown me, and continues to show me, His immense power and might through the application of this very scripture and it results in me viewing whatever situation I'm placed in or faced with from the proper perspective; through God's eyes!

Finding my strength in the Lord and both relying and trusting Him to be the source of my strength has been one of the most difficult and continuous lessons that I've had to learn, yet it is sincerely one of the most vital ones that we must apply and hold on to in our journey and walk with Christ.

Jozelle Luopu, Facebook-2014

*"I've learned to view every obstacle in my life as just another opportunity for God to let His glory shine. Contrary to popular belief, things have not always been smooth sailing, but a smooth sea has never made a skillful sailor and the Lord has made a way, every.single.time!"* <3

#GreatIsThyFaithfulness
#ForeverGrateful
- Zelle

Yes, the Lord has and continues to bless me with great and mighty things and opportunities, and as I praise Him for them all I can also say is that it is indeed the struggles, set-backs, heartbreaks and delays that He allowed, that led me into true worship. I realize and recognize that the very difficulties I experienced have had, and will always have purpose, not only to overcome the situation and circumstances at hand, but with the intent of strengthening my own personal relationship with my Heavenly Father!

As overcomers, The Lord desires for us to be unwavering in finding our refuge and strength in *Him!*

## Question:

How has the Lord showed you that you couldn't accomplish a particular goal/pursuit or overcome a circumstance without His help and without surrendering to His leadership?

_____

_____

_____

_____

_____

## *Prayer*

*Dear Lord, thank you for your divine strength; the strength that you bestow upon me. Thank you for your patience with me as I grow and learn the importance of surrendering to you, for you are my strong tower and in you I am able to overcome any and every hurdle and obstacle.*

*Where I am weak, you are strong.*

*In Jesus mighty name I pray, Amen.*

# DELIVERANCE AND RESTORATION

## DELIVERANCE AND RESTORATION
*March 14th, 2019 @ 9:45am*

I don't know why it both feels and seems as though there are people and/or spirits that just don't want to see me succeed!

But Satan has indeed Got. The. Wrong. One!

Whatever the enemy is up to in the spirit, for sure all it will do is make me an even better, stronger, more confident child and advocate of God. The enemy has indeed made thee biggest mistake! Know this!

I declare full and complete healing over my body, maturity in my faith and that all of God's promises to me be fulfilled in Jesus Name!

This is all a huge thrust in my faith. Purposefully a true test to both strengthen and increase the maturity of my trust in The Lord.

This is like a sling shot…being pulled back just a little bit, both briefly and intensely, with a purpose and as preparation to TAKE OFF, moving forward, suddenly and with a vengeance!

Also, I bless God how this situation, this spiritual battle, has mightily motivated my entire immediate family and encouraged them to strengthen their own personal relationship with their Heavenly Father! Not only teaching us how to war in the spirit, but also drawing us all deeper into prayer, fasting and studying the Word of God, which is our sword.

The enemy will NOT win, for he has already lost and through Christ, I. Am. Victorious!

**- KHAFA**

## Confidence in Christ

In the beginning of 2019, it was clearly revealed and confirmed to my family by way of the Holy Spirit that the physical complications that I had been experiencing in silence that had begun to drastically affect my daily living, was not at all the effects of a physical complication. After months and months of tests, scans and exams, no doctor or physician could find any reason or cause for what I was experiencing; they were all baffled. It was exposed and confirmed by way of the Holy Spirit that what I was actually experiencing were the physical effects of an intentionally targeted demonic attack on my life, devastatingly by someone close to me, and it required intense deliverance.

I must say, the entire experience was initially and completely terrifying because for the first time in my life, my eyes were opened to the fact that not everything and everyone is as it or they seem. Not everyone that smiles at you truly has good intentions for you. I am naturally a very trusting individual, sometimes too trusting, so it was all needed for my eyes to be opened to this truth and for me to begin seeking the Lord intensely for the gift of *discernment;* but that truth was also heartbreaking.

*"For our struggle is not against flesh and blood [contending only with physical opponents], but against the rulers, against the powers, against the world forces of this [present] darkness, against the spiritual forces of wickedness in the heavenly (supernatural) places. Therefore, put on the complete armor of God, so that you will be able to [successfully] resist and stand your ground in the evil day [of danger], and having done everything [that the crisis demands], to stand firm [in your*

*place, fully prepared, immovable, victorious]."*
**Ephesians 6:12-13**

What I was experiencing was another true *test*. The Lord never said that as His children we wouldn't experience hardships, but that He would never leave our side, and that as He wills it, we would come out on the other side, greater, stronger, more joyous, and lacking nothing!

> *"Consider it nothing but joy, my brothers and sisters, whenever you fall into various trials. Be assured that the testing of your faith [through experience] produces endurance [leading to spiritual maturity, and inner peace]. And let endurance have its perfect result and do a thorough work, so that you may be perfect and completely developed [in your faith], lacking in nothing."*
> **James 1:2-4 AMP**

Faith truly is, not simply *believing that God can*, but *knowing that He will!*

In this season, I realized that that the Lord was not only strengthening my endurance, but also ensuring that I grabbed hold of the concept and the importance of *Spiritual Warfare*. This test solidified my *confidence in Him* with a purpose to prepare me for the greatness that lies ahead, as well as the possible plots and plans of the enemy, that will fail every single time, because of it.

*New levels can also potentially bring 'new devils' as well.*

The Lord needed me to go deeper in Him, and what better way than to allow such a test, to not only open my eyes to what we are truly fighting in the spirit realm. Before this test I didn't have a full understanding of the fight in the spirit, but through this test I was thrusted into a lifestyle of passionately studying His Word and ensuring that I stood *firm* in it. *His word, the Bible, is the sword!*

*Above all, lift up the [protective] shield of faith with which you can extinguish all the flaming arrows of the evil one. And take the helmet of salvation, and the sword of the spirit, which is the Word of God.*
**Ephesians 6:16-17 AMP**

Along with the blessed assistance of some incredible men and women of God, I learned how to overcome; how to stand in the authority vested in me by my Lord and Savior, Jesus Christ, and how to fervently declare total deliverance, healing, restoration and renewal of my body, my mind, my memory and my speech, all of the areas that the enemy tried to attack and take from me. And what did our Heavenly Father do? Over time, He healed me from the crown of my head to the soles of my feet; restoring and renewing all of my senses, even better than they were, prior! The test was not to allow the enemy to win. The fact of the matter is that Satan already knows that *he is defeated,* and the Lord was once again able to demonstrate His unfailing power!

This season of my life gave me an enlightened understanding of our overall growth in Christ as believers.

Once we have chosen to walk with Him, our entire walk with the Lord is a constant process and journey of growth, correction, and strengthening in order to better prepare us for what's to come. It's not always an easy process, and don't let anyone fool you, there will be times when we sincerely feel like throwing in the towel. God is both allowing and using those rough patches, those valley's, to urge us to press forward, even if we feel as though we are holding on with everything we've got, ensuring that, just as the woman in the book of Matthew who had suffered for 12 years reached out with all that she had to touch the fringe of Jesus' robe, that we are doing the very same.

Not only trusting the Lord to save us, in spite of all the attempts of the enemy to make us succumb to defeat and disappointment, but to fearlessly stand firm and confident in The Lord, believing that not only will our current situation not last forever, but also, all that was broken and affected in the process will surely be restored.

We have to believe in the unsurpassable power of Jesus Christ; confident that the Lord's word will never return void.

*"So will My word be which goes out of My mouth;*
*It will not return to Me void (useless, without result),*
*Without accomplishing what I desire,*
*And without succeeding in the matter for which I sent it."*
**Isaiah 55:11 AMP**

To God be ALL the glory!

**Question:**

What is one mighty way that Lord has showed you that the power of prayer has the ability to turn the seemingly impossible completely around for your good and for His glory?

_____

_____

_____

_____

_____

**\*Prayer\***

*Dear Lord, thank you for your divine hedge of protection and for continually proving to us that ultimately the battles we face are indeed not ours, but yours, and therefore they are already won, by you! Thank you for using every evil plot and plan of the enemy simply as fuel to strengthen me, as you turn it all around for my good, and for your glory. May my tests result in mind blowing testimonies that continue to aid in the winning of souls for your kingdom.*

*In Jesus mighty name I pray, Amen.*

**LOVE**

## LOVE
*February 16th, 2017 @ 8:02pm*

"I never felt this way about someone. I have nowhere else to go- she is my home. She's the one I think about for everything I do. She's the reason why I want to be happy, so she can be next to someone who is happy - so that she can be happy too."

I watched this video segment on YouTube entitled, *"CBC, Hello Goodbye Canada - Lionel and Mary,"* and I cried true tears!

Seriously though, all of my life thus far, that is how I've always felt love should be. I was truly blessed to be raised with love like ***that***—it's all I know. And honestly, it's all I want to know.

*Love should feel like home.*

Of course, there will be difficulties, ups and downs, misunderstandings, miscommunications, hills and valley's etc., but in the end the goal is always to make it work. You fight for it because your love for one another isn't superficial nor is it circumstantial.

True love, real love, is so deep. True love, God's way, is a tag-team ministry within itself. You minister to each other first and in order to do that both parties must be committed to serving one another. It can't be solely about "what will I receive?" It must be about "how can I help, love, serve and assist in their growth? How can I be what God needs me to be for this individual who was divinely handpicked and placed in my life for such an incredible purpose? Both parties must have this perspective.

And because I've grown to love everything about love, most importantly that God is love, I would honestly rather be single and wait on the Lord to send the right one, who has the heart to love me properly, than to simply settle for anything less than God's best for me.

My heart wouldn't even allow me to.

My God wouldn't allow me to.

**- KHAFA**

God blessed me with one of the most amazing earthly blueprints of what true love between a man and a woman looks like. I was raised with parents who are undeniably, the very best of friends, a true power couple. It was God who brought them together and after years of hearing their love story, over and over, it's more than evident that it's the Lord who has been the glue that has held them together. They met at very young ages, both with their own histories and their own struggles, and many things such as distance and personal decisions could have broken their bond, but never did!

I honestly believe that it was what God knew I needed to grow up seeing, to ensure that the upcoming, fluctuating years of disappointment, growing pains and confusion that would follow, would never allow my heart and mind to opt- out of envisioning and believing the reality that true love between a husband and wife does exist, can beautifully thrive and also serve a purpose even greater than solely their feelings for one another!

I'm eternally grateful to God because every environment that *He* placed me in was where I needed to be and what I needed to see, when I needed to see it.

A blessed understanding of the Lord is that at times, He will simply allow us to stand back and be a witness to how something is done, in order to learn what to do as well as what *not* to do. He has surely allowed me, by His grace, to *observe* how a number of things have been done, and why He does not desire for them to be done that way.

That wasn't *always* the case for me though because at times I found myself not as an observer, but rather a partaker in those lessons.

Over time, it became evident that the Lord knew that *love* was an area that I was unfortunately going to learn the 'hard way', often due to my own poor choices and free will, but that in the end, I would be all the better for it as I would learn just how He desires for us to go about it. Though all of our paths will differ and be unique, as children of God we are still led by the spirit of God on how to walk through all that we're faced with, God's way.

> *"But He knows the way that I take [and He pays attention to it]. When He has tried me, I will come forth as [refined] gold [pure and luminous]."*
> **Job 23:10 AMP**

And tried/tested, He sure did! To be honest, it's not as if I left God with much of a choice, seeing as I certainly didn't seek Him first, nor did I even bother to test the waters. I allowed my emotions to lead me and jumped into this thing called 'love' at the tender age of 17, head and heart first!

In the beginning, it felt like an answered prayer that I don't even believe I had ever quite prayed for yet. And I must say, years later, I was able to see the blessing as well as the purpose in the midst of all the pain. At the time, however, it felt like pure punishment from the God whom I hardly ever reached out to unless I felt something was going wrong or contrary to how I felt it should be going in my life. I literally thought I could *use* God as a life saver, and though I gave the recommendation to others constantly to "pray about it" and would hastily google a few bible verses to share with those who came to me to vent their issues, I never truly took the time to read and study those bible verses and the context in which they were written, *for myself.*

When I was struggling in school or in a particular class is when

I could be found on my knees at the edge of my bed in tears, more so *begging* than actually *communing* with God. I had no real idea of who I was actually speaking to. So, when the relationship that I wholeheartedly was convinced would last forever, ended, there I was once again, on my knees in tears for years talking to my Heavenly Father. The father whom I still failed to acknowledge in *all* of my ways.

> *In all your ways know and acknowledge and recognize Him,*
> *And He will make your paths straight and smooth [removing*
> *obstacles that block your way].*
> **Proverbs 3:6 AMP**

For the first time ever, I truly experienced what heartbreak felt like. The kind of heartbreak that resulted in physical pain. It overtook practically every aspect of my life in that season.

1. My Health: I had a bad habit of overeating under stress and continually gained enormous amounts of weight as my stress increased, which also began to affect my bones, joints and my overall health, and as a result, my self-esteem.
2. My Focus: Focusing on the things I needed to do from day to day, especially studying while away in college, became the ultimate struggle for me because I was literally consumed by hurt, confusion and internal loneliness. I learned later that heartbreak, for me, was one of the biggest distractions the enemy tried to use to constantly take me off course.

When we're looking for things to distract us from hurt and pain, or just things we don't want to think about, it's not hard to find them. Satan is always lurking, ready and willing to make the search easy. I easily found myself involved in things that gave me nothing but temporary happiness, when what I was truly trying to do was fill a void that no earthly person, place or thing could ever fill! And though it took me years to understand and accept this, by the grace of God I finally came to the realization that the individual that I experienced both love and heartbreak with was not at all wicked or selfish, we were simply both young, had our own battles and both had a *great deal* to learn about ourselves, about love and about life as a whole.

God used that pain to teach me a very important lesson that a woman like myself needed to learn and never ever forget. God used heartbreak and how He strategically brought me out of it to also show me that, yes, one day I will most certainly learn to love the man that He has for me, *at the right time* and *the right way,* but that my heart must first and forever be rooted and grounded in *His* love!

*"May He grant you out of the riches of His glory, to be strengthened and spiritually energized with power through His Spirit in your inner self, [indwelling your innermost being and personality], 17 so that Christ may dwell in your hearts through your faith. And may you, having been [deeply] rooted and [securely] grounded in love, 18 be fully capable of comprehending with all the saints (God's people) the width and length and height and depth of His love [fully experiencing that amazing, endless love]; 19 and [that you may come] to know [practically, through personal experience] the love of Christ which far surpasses [mere] knowledge [without experience], that you may be filled up [throughout your being] to all the fullness of God [so that you may have the richest experience of*

*God's presence in your lives, completely filled and flooded with God Himself].*"
**Ephesians 3:16-19 AMP**

As I began to take a step back and look over my life, I became astounded at just how unworthy of God's love I truly was, yet, in my confusion and mess, *He still kept me!*

Many poor decisions I made and yet, *He continued to provide for me and protect me* even when I didn't acknowledge His presence or His faithfulness. I continually made the same mistakes over and over again, got the same results and still hadn't turned to Him for true guidance; yet, *He still pursued me!*

*God's ultimate demonstration of His love for us is Jesus Christ!*

*"But God clearly shows and proves His own love for us, by the fact that while we were still sinners, Christ died for us."*
**Romans 5:8 AMP**

The Lord is the epitome of Love, and the ultimate blue print of it. The fact is that no earthly being is capable of demonstrating, applying and exemplifying true love in such a perfect form and fashion. Not only is God the creator of love; *God Is Love!*

I looked over my life and saw just how flawless God's faithfulness is through His undeniable *patience* with me and His patience with me also became a daily demonstration of His unconditional love for me!

His love for me gave me clarity and instruction of the love I am to both give, as well as receive!

Being the promise keeping God that He is, at the perfect time, *His* perfect time, one of the biggest desires of my heart manifested.

*"Delight yourself in the Lord, and He will give you the desires and petitions of your heart."*
**Psalms 37:4 AMP**

He reminded me that I was never ever *forgotten* (what the enemy wanted me to believe) but that I am purposefully *set-apart* for His glory. For this reason, my journey and emotional experiences were consumed with hills and valley's that He allowed as lessons and *preparation* for His perfect will to be established is my life. He refused to allow me to solidify a permanent union with just anyone, but with the man He knew could and would properly lead.

The love and undeniable bond between my husband and I came together like a divine puzzle put together by God!

The Lord knew the desires of both of our hearts. He knew both what we wanted, and most importantly, what we both needed as we continue our journeys, complete our divine assignments and walk in purpose, as one.

*Trust the process; Trust His timing.*

God shall remain the foundation of a union pieced together by Him and shall forever be a priority of both parties. His blueprint of love for this world (the Bible) is the perfect instruction manual for how His children are to properly love and appreciate the special one that He has strategically handpicked for them.

*"Love endures long and is patient and kind; love never is envious nor boils over with jealousy, is not boastful or vainglorious, does not display itself haughtily. It is not conceited (arrogant and inflated with pride); it is not rude (unmannerly) and does not act unbecomingly. Love (God's love in us) does not insist on its own rights or its own way, for it is not self-seeking; it is*

*not touchy or fretful or resentful; it takes no account of the evil done to it [it pays no attention to a suffered wrong]. It does not rejoice at injustice and unrighteousness, but rejoices when right and truth prevail. Love bears up under anything and everything that comes, is ever ready to believe the best of every person, its hopes are fadeless under all circumstances, and it endures everything [without weakening]."*
**1 Corinthians 13:4-7 AMP**

*Waiting on the Lord to do things His way, is never in vain; I can proudly say that I am a living testimony of this!*

*To God be ALL the glory!*

**Question:**

The God we serve is indeed a jealous God, in which He makes no apologies for! Has there ever been a time when you found yourself putting your devotion to something or someone above your devotion and commitment to your love for the Lord?

_____

_____

_____

_____

_____

How did the Lord graciously humble you in order to get you back into proper alignment with Him?

_____

_____

_____

_____

## *Prayer*

*Most gracious and merciful God, thank you; for your love surpasses all understanding and is comparable to no other. I am undeserving of your love, yet you never seize to pour out and bestow it upon me! As I continue to grow in you, may your love for me forever remain the blueprint of how I properly exemplify your love to all those that I'm blessed to have a special bond with, as well as with those whose paths may temporarily yet purposely cross my path. May your light and love be shown in and through me here on earth, in all that I do.*

*In Jesus mighty name I pray, Amen.*

# CONCLUSION

## Be More Sincere

*"I've inquired about your love through the years; I've often
wondered why I'm here. Finding consolation through my tears,
**my one desire is to be more sincere...!"***
**– Song: Bless My Soul by Marcus Cole**

From the very moment I heard it, this song blessed me in a
mighty way. The words, "my one desire is to be more sincere"
overtook my heart in such a powerful way. It expressed the
exact feeling that came over me; the increased desire within my
heart to be more *sincere* about drawing closer to the Lord, getting
to *actually* know Him, and *truly* love Him; to be *real* about my
faith in Him.

About a year before I fully surrendered and decided with
my heart to give my life to Christ, I attended a church service
in Maryland with a group of my closest friends at the time. As I
walked up to the front of the church to be prayed with, I was all
smiles on the outside, but my heart was immensely heavy from
within and my mind was filled with so much confusion!

*"For God [who is the source of their prophesying] is not a God
of confusion and disorder but of peace and order. As [is the
practice] in all the churches of the saints (God's people)."*
*1 Corinthians 14:33 AMP*

A special Woman of God came up to me and prayed over me. I will
never forget that as she prayed, she continued to very peacefully yet
confidently and repetitively utter the words, *"may it drop from your
head to your heart!"* It amazed me at that very moment because

those words expressed the struggle I somehow felt from within but couldn't place into words until I heard her speak them.

From our *heads* to our *hearts*.

It was then that I encountered the Holy Spirit for the very first time!

But that was just the very beginning! We know, for example, as our understanding and trust for another human being grows, so does our love for them. It was absolutely no different for me, yet far better, as my love for the Lord began to overflow. The more my love for Him grew, the more I naturally felt inclined to say "not my will, but Lord, your will be done!"

My desire to draw nearer and nearer to God in sincere prayer increased. My prayers turned into true communing; it was as if I was literally conversing with one of my closest friends.

I was no longer waiting until something trying or tragic happened. I was actually *looking forward* to talking to my Heavenly Daddy and over time, I also learned how vital it was to *listen* for the voice of the Lord. I realized that yes, we as children of God must take the time to listen to our Heavenly Father. He both can and will speak to us in a way in which we can understand in order to further lead and guide us in the right direction!

All of this takes *time*.

Like any and everything in our lives that is a true priority to us, it's imperative that time, attention and effort be put forth and devoted by us, as well as a sincere desire within our hearts for a strong bond with our Heavenly Father to be built and maintained.

## God-given character

I was also given advice years ago by my Auntie Korlu, as she began to encourage me in my walk with Christ:

*"Do not let people force you to completely change your God-given personality, simply let the Lord work on your content and your character."*

What I took from that was, though I had given my life to Christ and was now living for the Lord, that didn't mean I needed to change the personality type He gave me; the outgoing and personable woman that I am. I didn't need to all of a sudden become someone who was always serious, who didn't like to have fun with those He placed in my life. I didn't need to quiet my laugh with those whose paths crossed mine or hold back from enjoying the beautifully blessed life He had given me!

In all honesty that was my first ignorant assumption of how I needed to begin carrying myself, but by the grace of God, He quickly placed me amongst an incredibly faith-filled and also very real, and down to earth church family that helped teach me how to seek God through His Word for myself. I sought Him from an authentic place and with less of a traditional and religious view. It was through that process that the Lord Himself began to work on my heart, which began to change my *decision making*. Conviction allowed me to see my thoughts, my words and my actions from a different perspective and also opened my eyes to how the things I did either represented or didn't represent the Lord and the Kingdom of God; things I truthfully never thought too deeply about before! The Lord also ensured that He instilled *wisdom* within me on how He desires for me to carry myself. He showed me how to recognize when I may actually be "doing the most" or being "extra" at a particular time and needed to quickly put myself *in check*. By realizing that boundaries are also needed, I am led to receive wise counsel and read and study The Word more and more so that I can properly apply God's instructions and wisdom. It also illuminated my love for Jesus and my understanding of the vital role that He plays in my life. The fact of the matter is that He is the only one who ever did and ever will live a perfect life. No one will ever be blameless, none of us can be *good enough, long enough!*

When Christ died, His righteousness was passed down to us.

*He who earnestly seeks righteousness and loyalty*
*finds life, righteousness, and honor.*
**Proverbs 21:21**

To this day, I am the God-fearing, laughter-filled and fun-loving woman I was created to be. I believe He uses the personality He blessed me with to naturally be more relatable to others in a way that allows them to feel comfortable opening up about their own hills and valleys of life, which in turn allows a pathway for sincere encouragement and the truth and goodness of God to be shared.

We're all created unique by God, and as His children, have the purpose of sharing the Good News with those around us and winning souls for Christ!

May we either begin to, or continue to allow our Heavenly Father to work on us from the inside out, molding and rebuilding the areas of our lives that may have somehow crumbled, to ensure that we grow comfortable and proud of who He has destined us to be so that the light of Christ is shown in and through us to the areas of the world that are dark.

He doesn't desire to override who He beautifully and strategically created us to be. He intends to use all the good within us to glorify His name and lead others to the greatest love they will ever know, *Jesus Christ.*

*I found true peace, solace, pure joy and excitement in the realization that all of this takes place by God's grace, as I am constantly evolving, and steadily revolving...*

*...In my Father's Arms*

## Prayer of Salvation

*God, I recognize that I have not lived my life for You up until now. I have been living for myself and that is wrong. I need You in my life; I want You in my life. I acknowledge the completed work of Your Son Jesus Christ in giving His life for me on the cross at Calvary, and I long to receive the forgiveness you have made freely available to me through this sacrifice. Come into my life now, Lord. Take up residence in my heart and be my king, my Lord, and my Savior. From this day forward, I will no longer be controlled by sin, or the desire to please myself, but I will follow You all the days of my life. Those days are in Your hands. I ask this in Jesus' precious and holy name, Amen. "*

CPSIA information can be obtained
at www.ICGtesting.com
Printed in the USA
LVHW020510180720
661006LV00018B/741